A FUNNY THING HAPPENED ON THE WAY TO SENILITY

Jerry Page

 iUniverse®

A FUNNY THING HAPPENED ON THE WAY TO SENILITY

iUniverse books may be ordered through booksellers or by contacting:

iUniverse
1663 Liberty Drive
Bloomington, IN 47403
www.iuniverse.com
844-349-9409

ISBN: 978-1-6632-0559-9 (sc)
ISBN: 978-1-6632-0560-5 (e)

Print information available on the last page.

iUniverse rev. date: 08/13/2020

The jokes contained in this timeless tome span at least the last 50 years. I really don't recall what I had for dinner last night, but I remember jokes that I heard in grade school. When faced with a desire to write something, I went with what I had to offer. Jokes.

There was a period in the late fifties through the late sixties that will have to remain where they are as they are kinda on the politically incorrect side. One needs to take the advice given to whales which comes down to, "If you don't spout off, you don't get harpooned".

There are two words that need to be discussed before the joke writing begins, one is a euphemism for sex and the other is a euphemism for feces. I was torn between letting the chips fall where they may and use them both in an unedited manner or edit them in a manner that would not render the jokes unfunny. I have come up with a solution that will work for both factions. I am going to use both words in an unedited manner, with the option for proper self-editing by anyone who is offended by the language to use a felt tip pen and a short amount of time Hopefully people read this and not be blindsided by the "f-bombs".

If one does some historic research, they will find that the word "shit" did not begin with the negativity associated with it at this point in time.

When the colonies in Massachusetts were first settled, the main industry was farming, but by the end of the second harvest, it was a certainty that the native soil would not support growing crops.

Someone opined that what they lacked were the herds of milk cows that flourished in England. The cows had one byproduct that was sadly lacking in the new world, and that byproduct was a nuisance as well as a blessing. The cows produced cow manure is massive quantities, usually in the barn during milking. Someone came up with the idea that rather than import a sizeable quantity of cows, all they needed was a yearly supply of cow manure. And by that very idea, an entire new supply system was born.

In what could only be described as a remarkably short period of time, a new industry came into being. There was one notable problem that wasn't apparent until everything was organized and the first sailing ships were at the docks waiting for product. Nobody could be found that would man the ships without better pay. The famers would not pay more than the agreed upon shipping rate, and experienced sailors had plenty of work without hauling, and being exposed to raw cow manure. The manpower shortage was solved one evening as two of the ship captains were engaged in some spirited drinking at one of the local watering holes. At first, they were annoyed by the noise and confusion caused by tables of young men who one by one, would pass out and be dragged out into the alley behind the bar.

Within a few weeks, a new business venture went into action.

The crews of the ships would go into the local bars in the evening, and buy round after round of drinks for the local young bucks. When they had been carried out to the alley and deposited on the ground, the rest of the crew hauled them to the docks and placed them on the deck of the ship that was going to sea early in the morning.

Many a young man awoke in the throes of his first hangover, upon opening their eyes, they all had the same questions for whomever the saw. "Where am I, why is the ground moving, and what stinks?" Over the next few years, some ships never made it to the colonies and it was a mystery that was solved as, one day in Boston harbor, a ship moored offshore exploded. That is when they discovered that cow manure produced an explosive compound called methane.

It was reasoned that they needed to have air circulating around the odiferous cargo, so therefore put up shelves to keep the air circulating around the precious freight and vented out of the cargo hold.

As a visual reminder to keep the cargo ventilated, the shippers came up with a ploy that seemed to work. On the top of every box of the fragrant cargo, they stenciled the words, "Stow high in transit" as this was fairly time consuming, they decided to abbreviate the warning with the following, "SHIT".

To the best of my knowledge, this is a true account, if it isn't true, I blew the price of one beer to an old guy that attested to its veracity.

Now let's explore the other four-letter word that we need to deal with.

In the last thirty or so years, the word F**K has become ubiquitous, it's everywhere and has little shock factor left. There are, however people that take great offense to its use. To those folks, I have used the F-bombs thinly disguised as per the beginning of this paragraph.

As a casual suggestion, why not just get a black felt tip pen and do your own editing. It will not require a lot of time or level of expertise, and will give you a warm feeling to have beaten the system. In fact, it reminds me of some graffiti I encountered in a truck stop restroom.

It went like this: "Doing a good job here is like wetting your pants in a dark suit, it gives you a temporary warm feeling, but nobody seems to notice."

You may also have noticed that there is no table of contents at the start of this timeless volume, the reason being all lines would be the same, "Page 23 - Joke", "Page 24 – Joke", it seemed like a no brainer to leave it out. (Note to editor- If necessary, feel free to go with the table of contents)

As a frame of reference, I will admit that even though I am a licensed surveyor, I did actually drive semi's a million miles in 47 states. Both of those backgrounds contributed fairly evenly to content being regurgitated herein.

Although there is no table of contents, I gave each joke a more or less description.

OK here we go......

JOKES

A man had been experiencing a considerable amount of pain in his left shoulder. His wife finally nagged him to being desperate enough to finally consent to visiting the doctor. The doctor gave him a cursory examination, and handed him a small plastic jar complete with a lid, and instructed him to return on the following Tuesday with a urine specimen. This prompted him to inquire whether the doctor had been paying attention as it was his shoulder, which seemed to him not really connected to urine output. The doctor ensured him that Serology was an exact science and would provide the answer concerning his shoulder issues. He returned home and thinking he was being charged considerable money for useless lab tests, decided to mess with the doctor. He put a little bit of urine in the cup, and his wife put in a little as well as his teenage daughter. As the final act he followed his dog around the back yard until the dog contributed also. (It should be noted here that it was two months before he and the dog made eye contact again.) On the appointed Tuesday, he returned the urine specimen and was given a follow up appointment in one week.

Upon entering the doctor's office, he was confronted by the doctor poring over his test results while frowning and muttering to himself. "Doc, what's wrong? He asked". The doctor looked up at him, and replied "You know I really used to believe in this shit, do what they told me from your urine specimen? I'll tell you what. "They say that your wife is pregnant, your daughter has an STD and your dog has distemper, not only that but if you don't quit playing with yourself, your shoulder will break down."

1

WESTERN UNION

Back not long after the great depression, a young man who had grown up on a farm in the Midwest moved to a big city and found employment with Western Union delivering telegrams. After a few months, his co-workers discovered that he was a virgin. They took up a collection and hired a hooker for him as a surprise. They gave him a dummy telegram and her address for delivery. He arrived at the apartment address and knocked on the door. The door opened to a naked woman, who grabbed him by the shirt while saying, "Quick, come in, I hear somebody coming." With the door closed, she wrapped her arms around him and asked, "Tell me, big boy, what do you think would be the most sensitive part of my body"" After a short hesitation, he replied "Ma'am, it's got to be your ears." "My ears?"" Why would you possibly say my ears?" Well Ma'am, he replied, when you said that you heard someone coming, it was me."

MICKEY'S DIVORCE

It was a sad day indeed, Mickey and Minnie are in divorce court and Mickey is on the witness stand, "Let me get this straight, Mr. Mouse", asked the judge, "your grounds for divorce is insanity?" Mickey replied "I didn't say she was crazy, your honor, I said she was F**king Goofy."

THE FARMER'S NEW WIFE

A young farmer called the local farm implement supply company and inquired about purchasing a milking system. The first question concerned the size of his herd. When he replied that he only had one cow, the salesman asked why he would go to that expense for only one cow. The young farmer said that he had newly gotten married, when they arrived at his farm, after a brief honeymoon, the new bride stayed in the house while he went to the barn to milk the cow. He had barely started to milk when the cow hit him on the side of his head with a tail coated with cow manure. He yelled at the cow, but cows are stubborn creatures and the yelling had little effect as five minutes later she repeated the assault. This time he had had enough and decided to fix the issue. He found a piece of bailing twine and tied the cow's tail to the low hanging rafter of the barn while standing on the milking stool to accomplish the task. Just as the task was finished, his belt broke, his pants fell down just as his new bride walked into the barn. Then and there she took over the milking chores.

TRUCK STOP HOOKER

This is a true account that I found quite humorous, I was laid over one night and parked in the parking lot of a Truckstop in Houston, Texas. It was a pretty typical evening with an endless stream of bullshit on the CB. A quite attractive blond girl was wandering around the parking lot and appeared to be plying the world's oldest profession. Pretty soon the girl was the main source of conversation on the radio, and a little later she was talking on some driver's CB. Another driver asked her what her price would be, and she replied that her price was $100. That was quite high compared to normal for that period of time, so the driver said that for that kind of money they would have to do it his way. She inquired as to the nature of "his way" and received the reply. 'On credit'.

MOVING TO AUSTRALIA

A man storms into his house one afternoon, goes up to his wife and exclaims quite loudly, "I'm sick of this town, and sick of my job, and sick of this house, and I'm sick of being with you, I'm leaving". He runs up the stairs and slams the door to their bedroom. After a few minutes, she enters the bedroom and sees that he is packing his suitcase. "Where are you going?" she inquires. His reply was, "I moving to Australia". "What are you going to do for a living in Australia"? she asked. Without hesitation he replies, "I heard today that there are plenty of women there that would pay a man like me, $20 for sex. A little later he notices that she is also packing her suitcase. "Where are you going" he asks. "To Australia", she replies. "Why would you want to go to Australia", he asked. "I want to see you try to live on $40 a month."

LIGHT BEER

Do you know why light beer is like making love in a canoe?

They are both f**king near water.

SAM THE COOK

A young man gets employed herding cattle on a long cattle drive. After a couple of weeks, he approaches the trail boss and asks if there are any towns in the immediate area. The foreman replies in the negative. He senses that the young cowboy is ready for some action the local area can't produce, namely hookers. He replies that he knows what the young man is after, but the only source of relief is old Sam the cook. The cowboy is quite taken aback by the whole idea and replies. "No way, I don't go for that shit." After a month or so, he approaches the trail boss one more time and is offered the same advice. The trail boss told him all he needed to do was get 3 or 4 of the other cowboys and go see old Sam. His reply was, "Why do I need 3 or4 guys to go with me. The trail boss replied, "old Sam don't go for that shit neither".

PLAY CARNIVAL

Over heard on CB radio: A trucker asks a woman if she would like to play "carnival", She asked how to play the game, to which he replied, "You come sit on my face, and I'll try to guess your weight".

POSTUM

To make this work for anyone under 50 or so, I need to explain that Postum was a wheat-based coffee substitute.

A man received a prescription from his doctor for some suppositories, and was instructed to return in week to check on his progress. Upon returning to the doctor's office, he was asked how the prescription was working. He said, "Doc, these things don't work at all". When asked if he took them as prescribed on the label. He answered that he came as close as he could. When asked what that entailed, he replied, "It said to insert in rectum, I didn't have any of that, so I put them in my Postum, and not only do they taste terrible, but for all the good they did, I might as well as stuck them up my butt."

BAD DAY TO HITCH-HIKE

A slightly deranged young woman loved the smell of burning rubber, so every time she came to a stop sign, she would speed up and then at the last second, would slam on the brakes, roll down her window and sniff the burning rubber. One afternoon as she was driving through the countryside, she stopped and picked up a hitch hiker, she drove for several miles and subsequently forgot about her passenger. A few miles down the road, she noticed a train that was approaching a crossing about ¼ mile ahead of her. She immediately accelerated to 70 mph and a collision appeared to be imminent. At the last second, she slammed on the brakes and broad-sided to a stop only a few feet short of the train that was already at the crossing. She rolled he window down and started inhaling the burning rubber. Just then a shaky voice from the back seat proclaimed, "You smell it lady, I'm sitting in it".

"NICE DOGGY"

Two slightly drunk men were sitting on a park bench one afternoon, when a dog came walking down the sidewalk, then laid down and started licking himself. One of the pair turned to the other, and stated, "wow, I wish I could do that." His buddy said, "well, go ahead, but you probably should pet him first."

BUCKET METHOD

A young sociologist was taking a survey in the hills of Kentucky, he was asking the locals about their preferred birth control method. He knocked on the door of a rundown looking cabin, and the door was answered by a young woman who was well over 6 feet in height. He explained the nature of his enquiry and asked her about the manner of birth control she and her spouse favored. Without hesitation, she stated that they used the bucket method. Having never heard of that method, he asked if she would please explain how that worked. She explained by stating, "My husband, Clem, is barely 5 feet tall, so we do it standing up, and Clem stands on a bucket. I watch him really close, and when his eyes start to cross, I kick the bucket out from under him."

ELEPHANT JOKES

Why does an elephant have four feet? Because 6 inches wouldn't work.

Why do elephants have flat feet" From jumping out of trees.

Why should you never go through the jungle between the hours of 2 and 4 in the afternoon? Because that's when the elephants practice jumping out of trees.

Why are there no alligators in the jungle? Because they insisted on going through the jungle between 2 and 4.

How do you tell that an elephant has been in your refrigerator? By the tracks in the jello.

What's gray and comes by the quart" Elephants.

Why was the elephant wearing red tennies? Because the blue ones were in the wash.

ARCHIE AND EDITH AT CHURCH

Edith Bunker, finally wheedled Archie into going to church one Sunday morning. At the end of the service the pastor informed the congregation that a group of travelling missionaries would be in town the following week and volunteers were needed to house and feed them. Hands were raised and promises made. When all the bases were covered, Edith raised her hand and volunteered to provide sex. As the congregation trooped out the door, the pastor turned to Edith and said, "Excuse me Mrs. Bunker, at first I thought that I heard you volunteer to provide sex." Edith confirmed that that was exactly what she had offered. When asked for further explanation, she stated that she wanted to do something and had asked Archie what she could do and he said, "F**k 'em".

RAISIN BREAD

There was a bakery in a small college town, that employed a beautiful young woman who worked behind the counter. She always wore very short skirts and a rumor started that she wore no underwear. Soon the local college guys started coming in to the bakery every morning, and always ordered whatever kind of bread that was on the top shelf of the rack next to the wall. She had to get the ladder, carry it over to the rack, then climb up to get the bread while the young guys stood at the bottom of the ladder and enjoyed the view. One morning the raisin bread was on the top rack, so naturally all the guys were ordering that. One morning a little old gentleman entered the bakery as she was at the top of the ladder and was taking in the view with a couple of the young guys. She noticed the newcomer and hoping to avoid another trip up the ladder, looked at the old guy and asked, "Is yours raisin too?" After a short pause, he admitted, "No, but it twitched a couple times."

THE NEW COOK

The cook at the cow camp suddenly died, and with no one else available for the job, the trail boss appointed one of the cowboys as the new cook. And as an aside, stated that the first guy that complained would be the new cook. The new cook actually did try at first, but hated the job, and knew that the only way to get out of it was to generate a complaint. He tried everything he could think of with no response. The other cowboys would go to great lengths not to complain. One afternoon out of desperation, he went out to the horse corral and picked up some horse poop, took it to the kitchen and put frosting on it. After dinner, he brought the "desert" out and put one on each plate. The first cowboy bit into the desert, and exclaimed, "This tastes like shit...., but good!

THE GOLDEN ANNIVERSARY

An elderly couple were contemplating their upcoming 50th wedding anniversary when the wife did some research and discovered that the chapel where they were married at Niagara Falls was still in business, as well as the restaurant where they dined and the hotel where they spent the wedding night. Arrangements and reservations were made, and on the anniversary, they went through the same ceremony, had the same dinner at the same restaurant, and retired to the same room. The only difference was that this time he complained that it was too big.

THE GORILLA

A huge male gorilla escaped from a large metropolitan zoo; it was several days before he was re-captured. He was found in the home of an older single woman, and had been holding her as a sex slave. After he was discovered and taken back to the zoo, there was much concern about the mental and physical wellbeing of the woman. Her oldest and dearest friend was the first one to offer her support. She gave her friend a hug, and tried to console her as best she could. The woman burst into tears and, said that it was just terrible. Then she added, "He never calls, he never writes".

COYOTE TRAP

Over a beer or six one evening the conversation turned to past painful experiences. After a while, one of the group's members finally spoke up. He allowed as how he could top all of the testimony to that point. When asked to explain, he told them that he had been out hunting with a bunch of guys, and left the campfire to go back into the brush to leave a deposit to nature, so to speak. He told about undoing his belt, then dropping his pants, and of squatting down to finish the job. However, when he squatted down his "love machine" tripped a coyote trap which snapped shut on said appendage. One of his companions allowed as that had to the worst pain in the world. He told them that although the pain was terrible, there was one pain that was worse. When asked what that could possibly be, he said it was when he got and started running and came to the end of the chain.

THE SPECIAL

There was a freight truck driver that had worked for the same company in the same town for many years. He always ran the same route, and also stopped at the same diner for lunch, and always ordered whatever the special of the day was. One Monday everything went wrong, the freight was loaded in the wrong order, as well as being delivered late. To add insult to injury, he had a flat tire halfway through the morning. The diner had run out of the special by the time he arrived and scratched it off the menu. He walked in, sat down on his favorite stool, and before he could order, one of the waitresses walked up with a smirk on her face, and told him that she knew what he wanted and had just scratched it. Without a pause, he replied, "Cool, now go wash your hands and bring me the special."

BAD DAY OF GOLF

A man was downtown one day heading for the hardware store, when he saw his best golfing buddy walking up towards him. He said, "Hey Charley, how are you doing?" Charley answered, "I'm doing OK." "Charley, what's wrong with your voice" "I really don't want to talk about it, if I tell you, you'll just laugh." The man replied, "C'mon Charley, we've been buddies for a long time and I'm concerned about you." Charley replied, "I was out at the course Sunday, and on the fifth hole, I sliced the ball really badly and it went into some trees. I walked around one of the trees and there was a cow, her back was humped up and her tail was up in the air. I looked and there was a golf ball up her butt". I looked over and there was this immense woman bent over looking for her golf ball, I held the cow's tail up and said, hey lady, does this look like yours? And the bitch hit me in the throat with a 5 iron".

A WORSE DAY OF GOLF

The guy in the previous account came home hours late from the golf course one Saturday. When his wife enquired as to the reason for being so late. He replied, "It was a terrible day, on the second tee, my buddy, Charley grabbed his chest and fell down dead." The wife agreed that it must have been a really horrible day. "You can't imagine, all day long it was hit the ball, drag Charley, hit the ball, drag Charley.

UNCLE BOB

A man and his 4-year-old son were driving home one Saturday, when the little boy looked over on the side of the street and spied two dogs engaged in making more dogs. "Daddy, look at that the lad shouted." "Yeah son, the dog on top has a hurt foot and the one on the bottom is helping him home." The son replied, "Wow that's just like what uncle Bob said" "What did uncle Bob say?" asked the father. The little guy said, "Do somebody a favor and they'll f**k you every time."

ANOTHER ROUND OF GOLF

Two elderly gentlemen were playing a leisurely round of golf on a Saturday afternoon. Neither of them had ever met the other, so the conversation was casual, with the occasional joke. As they prepared to tee off on the eighth hole, one of them noticed a funeral procession coming up the street beside the course. He walked over by the street and removed his hat and held it over his heart as the procession passed by. His companion complemented him for his show of concern. "Well, we would have been married for 46 years next month."

BLACK BELT

It was late one Saturday night in a tavern in a bad part of a large city. Most of the clientele were past middle age and showed signs of a mis-spent youth. They had obviously lived a tough life. A young man who was a stranger to the bar was getting quite drunk and obnoxious to boot. One of the locals, suggested that it might be in his best interest to sit down and shut up. At that, the young man stood up and looking the older gentleman in the eye, stated "C'mon old man, but let me warn you that I have a black belt." The older man opined, "you need to hold on to that belt." When asked what was meant by that last remark. The explanation was that it would come in handy for lowering him into the ground.

SLOE GIN

A teenage kid had become acquainted with the new neighbor next door to his home. After getting to know each other, the older guy asked if the kid would be interested in doing some chores around his place in exchange for some spending money. The boy readily agreed and arrangements were made for the following Saturday. It became a weekly thing; some task was completed in exchange for said money. One Saturday was hotter than usual, and the lad was sweating profusely by the time the lawn was mowed. His employer was seated in the back yard in the shade of a large tree when the kid came to collect. The neighbor asked if the kid would like a beer, never having experience beer before, but having heard all kinds of good things about it, readily agreed. The first taste of beer was not what he expected, in fact he refused to drink more than one sip. The neighbor looked through his cupboards and all he could find was a bottle of Sloe Gin. He mixed a drink with some lime juice and soda and offered it to his young neighbor. The kid liked it and subsequently drank several glasses full. About four hours later the youngster awoke on the couch in the neighbor's living room. He made it home without his folks seeing him, and went up to his room for another nap. The following week, after doing the chores for the new neighbor, he was asked if he would like a drink. He said it sounded good, but he didn't want any of that Sloe Gin. When asked what was his objection to the drink, he stated, "It made my butt hurt."

WILLY NELSON

A rather inebriated woman entered a tattoo parlor in Nashville. She told the tattoo artist that she wanted two tattoos. She wanted Elvis Pressley on the inside of one thigh, and Conway Twitty on the inside of the other thigh. When the job was finished, the tattoo artist handed her a mirror and after looking at the new tattoos, she refused to pay. She said that she couldn't tell which one was which. The artist tried to reason with her to no avail. As a last resort they came to an agreement. They would go out to the street and stop the first person they encountered, and would agree with what ever the opinion of that person would be. They had only gone part of a block, when they met a somewhat inebriated gentleman walking in their direction. When they met, she pulled up her skirt, and parted her thighs, and proceeded to ask his opinion of the two tattoos. After a brief hesitation, he said, "Well ma'am I don't know who the twins are, but the one in the middle looks like Willy Nelson.

OLD BULL + YOUNG BULL

Two range bulls were walking down a dusty trail out in the Summer range land. One was starting his first season as a range bull. His companion was a grizzled veteran of many summers. The young bull looked of in the distance and spotted a group of heifers beside the trail. "Hey" he exclaimed, "Lets run down there and breed a couple of those heifers". "No, son" said the old bull, "Let's walk down there and breed all those heifers".

 CHRISTMAS SPIRIT

It was the quintessential pre-Christmas lunch in the company lunchroom. One of the guys had enjoyed about as much Christmas cheer as he could stand and was making his point well known. One of his female co-workers tried to reason with him. She told him that he just didn't have the Christmas spirit. He looked her square in the eye, and stated, "Christmas spirit"? Let me tell you about Christmas spirit, last year I bought my wife a fur coat, and my son a new sports car. Do you know what I received in return" I got a pair of slippers, and a piece of ass, and they were both too big."

98 POUND WEAKLING

Many years ago, there were several monthly "men's" magazines that all had one thing in common. The thing was a section of men's only advertising at the very back of the magazine. One of the most prominent adds was for a body building course that showed a skinny "weakling" who got sand kicked in his face while some big body builder stole his girlfriend. Hence this next joke.

Did you hear about the 98-pound weakling that moved to Alaska? He came back a husky f**ker.

A DELICATE QUESTION

A young boy came up to his mother one afternoon, and asked her if pole dancers came apart. She asked him why he would ask a thing like that. He said that he had heard Daddy tell the guy next door that he would like to screw the ass off of one of them.

HEARING PROBLEM

A grizzled old cowboy walked into the waiting room at a small country town doctor's office. As he approached the receptionist at the front desk, she asked him the nature of his problem. He stated that that was what he needed to see the doctor about. She informed him that he had to tell her the nature of the problem, so she could inform the doctor. He said "well ma'am it's my pecker." There was suddenly silence in the waiting room and mothers had their hands over children's ears. The receptionist grabbed him by the front of his shirt and pulled him outside. She explained that for something of a delicate nature like that, he should tell her that it was something like a problem with his ear. She then told him to come back in and do it correctly. She resumed her seat and as he approached the desk asked what was the nature of his problem, and he stated that he had a problem with his ear. She asked what was wrong with his ear, and he stated, "I can't piss out of it."

SNORING PROBLEM

Four guys went hunting one fall, equipped with two pup tents for sleeping. The first morning as they were standing around the fire, one of them noticed that his buddy who had spent the night in the other pup tent didn't look like he felt very good. He took him aside and asked if he was having a problem of some sort. His buddy nodded in ascent and then told him the problem. The guy he was sleeping with snored all night long, and he hardly got any sleep at all. The first guy said that that wasn't an issue and that he would be happy to trade tents with him. The next morning the buddy asked the guy that had traded with him how he had slept. "I slept like a log", he stated. "you mean the snoring didn't keep you awake?" "He never snored" came the reply. His buddy couldn't help asking for some clarification on exactly how that all came about. He was told that just after he blew out the candle, the night before, he leaned over and patted the guy on the butt and kissed him in the ear, and he never closed his eyes all night.

THE ADMIRAL'S SECRET

A young man worked as an orderly for a grizzled old sea captain for several years. Every morning the old man would take a key out of a drawer, open a cabinet, take out a small wooden box, take out a piece of paper, read it while his lips were moving. Then replace the paper and put everything back the way it was. Dying of curiosity, the actions of the captain remained a mystery until one day the old man had a stroke and died. The orderly ran up to the captain's room and opened the box and read the paper, it said, "Port is left, and starboard is right."

LADY GODIVA

It's odd how some sayings that are widely used for decades, came into being. Take for example, "hooray for our side." To the best of my knowledge that saying can be traced back to Lady Godiva's historic ride. In those days, women always rode side saddle, and therefore one side of the street got a much better view than the other. This prompted one onlooker on the "good" side to exclaim, "Hooray for our side!!"

CLASS REUNION

A young man decided to attend a high school reunion. Not long after his arrival, he ran into an old high school sweetheart, whom he hadn't seen since graduation. They made some small talk about what they had been up to since the school days, over a few drinks. She inquired, "Are you married?" to which he replied, "No, not anymore." She responded with, "Wow, me too." "Why did you get divorced?" she asked. "She said that I was too kinky" he replied. "Wow, me too!" she exclaimed. A few more drinks and a couple hours later, they entered a motel room. She broke the silence with, "What do you want to do first?" To which he replied, "Pull your dress up over your head and go stand in that corner." This was a new one on her, she had never explored this corner of kinkiness. Nothing happened for several minutes, prompting her to ask what was going on. A short time later, he walked up to her and exclaimed, "Wow that was great!!" to which she asked, "What did you do?" To which he replied, "I shit in your purse".

THE ACTOR'S BIG BREAK

There was a young man who very much wanted to be a professional actor. He had hired an agent, and had played a lot of roles, but only off Broadway. One morning, he received a call from his agent, who told him of an offer for a part in a Broadway production, but wouldn't recommend taking it. When asked why not take it, the agent told him that it was a very small part, in fact it consisted of walking on stage, making a gesture, saying one line, and exiting the stage. He didn't care about the brevity of the part, it was his lifetime desire to act on Broadway, and this might be his only opportunity. It was decided that in the light of how minor the role was, and the fact that he had considerable experience, that he wouldn't have to travel to New York until the day that the play opened. He spent days on his part until he thought he had it mastered. The play was about medieval times, with castles and cannons. His only line required that he make a gesture, and utter the phrase, "Hark, that sounds like cannon fire". On the day of the opening, everything went wrong. His plane was late leaving, and had to circle the airport for a considerable amount of time before landing. To top it all off the cab that he took to the theatre broke down, and required a second cab, all of which took considerable time. He arrived at the theatre only a few minutes before he had to recited his part. He ran into the makeup dept. to get his costume and makeup on, before making a mad dash towards the stage. As he approached the stage manager pointed to him and pointed toward the stage. He ran out on stage, made his dramatic gesture, and just as he began his one line, a cannon went off right behind him which prompted his one line to be, "What the f**k was that?"

THE DIMMER SWITCH

There was once a married woman who decided the "magic" had vanished from the bedroom that she shared with her husband. After a short discussion, they agreed that each would do something to make their love making more romantic before bedtime that evening. For her part she bought a sexy negligee, he installed a dimmer switch in the bedroom.

MIND IF I CUT IN?

It was the morning of the weekly confessional for the nuns at the convent. One by one they waited their turn. The first one started off with, "Bless me Father, for I have sinned. "I have looked on the private parts of a man." Her penance was to say 50 Hail Marys and wash her eyes in the holy water. The next confessed to touching the private parts of a man, and instructed to say 60 Hail Marys and wash her hands in the holy water. This went on for some time and a while later there was a line of nuns waiting their turns at the holy water. The nun at the back of the line asked the nun in front of her if she could cut in before her. She said that she wanted to gargle before the other nun dipped her butt in the water.

DRUNK IN ELEVATOR

It was the last week before Christmas, and the shopping rush was in full swing. A young lady had been frantically trying to get the last of her shopping done before she had to be home to fix dinner. She got in the elevator on the fourth floor, and just as she was pushing the button to close the door, she had some stomach cramps and passed a considerable amount of gas. Hoping no one else would get on the elevator, she rummaged through her purchases and found the aerosol can of Christmas room deodorizer and sprayed the smell of pine trees all around the elevator. She had no more than finished with the task, when the elevator stopped, and a quite drunken man entered. After a brief pause, he muttered to himself. "Damn, it smells like somebody just shit a Christmas tree in here."

WRONG FIRST AID

A few friends went to the woods on the opening weekend of deer season. They had hunted in these woods many years and all had their own favorite places to hunt, so split up to hunt, and agreed to be back at camp before sunset. One of the guys was hunting by himself, and rounded a small group of trees, only to be confronted by a scene he could hardly believe. One of his buddies was bent over a log with his pants down around his ankles while he was being sexually molested by his hunting companion. "What the hell's going on here?" His buddy said, "oh man, this is awful, Wally had a heart attack." When asked why he wasn't applying mouth to mouth resuscitation. He replied, "How do think this got started.?

A RUN OF BAD LUCK

There once was a farmer in the Midwest who was enduring a horrendous run of bad luck. His wheat crop was failing, his only son and heir contracted a severe case of the mumps, and to save his life, had to be castrated, his wife ran off with a salesman, some hunters shot the balls off his prize bull, one afternoon as he sat in his living room, lightning stuck his house and set it on fire. Having reached the end of his rope, he ran out into the front yard, looked up at the heavens, and screamed, "why me?" The clouds parted and a big voice boomed out, "I don't know, there's just something about you that pisses me off."

SEX MAKES HAPPINESS

A psychologist had spent several years working to prove that the frequency of sex was directly related to happiness. He had gone to great lengths to show that men who had the most sex were happier. The first group of volunteers were brought to the stage, they all claimed to have sex at least once per day, they were the happiest guys you could ever hope to see. Then one by one the volunteers were replaced by men who got less and less sex. Each group was unhappier than the last. Finally, he came to the grand finale, he had found a man that claimed to only get sex once per year. When the man came out, he seemed happier than any of the preceding groups. You couldn't wipe the grin off his face with a two by four. The psychologist was dumbfounded, and asked the man why he was so happy. The young man exclaimed, "Tonight's the night!"

OFF THEIR ROCKERS

An elderly couple were sitting on their front porch one evening enjoying the summer weather. Suddenly the wife leaned over and knocked her husband out of his rocker. He picked himself up and got back into his chair, and demanded what had come over her. She replied, "that was for having such a small one." A short while later the husband leaned over and knocked his wife out of her rocker. After picking herself off the floor, she asked what that was for. He responded that it was for knowing the difference.

BEEN TO SPOKANE

An elderly couple were on a plane destined for the city of Reno. The husband was in the aisle seat. A little later the man in the seat across the aisle, reached over and tapped the husband on the shoulder, "Where you folks from?" he inquired. The husband told him that they lived in Spokane, Washington. The wife tugged on her husband's sleeve and wanted to know what the other man said. He told her about the brief conversation, resumed looking straight ahead. A little later the man across the aisle tapped the husband on the shoulder and confided, "I was in Spokane one night, met a woman there, and had the worst sex of my life." This time the wife grabbed him by the sleeve and demanded to know what the other man had said. The husband looked at her and said, "He thinks he knows you."

A LIMERICK

There was a young woman from Madras, who had a magnificent ass, not rounded and pink as you probably think, it was grey, had long ears, and ate grass.

WHERE YOU ALL FROM?

A young woman was in a bar in a strange city and decided to try to get into a conversation with the woman seated next to her. She inquired, "Where you all from? "she asked. The woman seemed to resent the intrusion, and told her that she was from a place where they don't end sentences with prepositions, and turned away. "Let me rephrase that" she said, "where you all from, bitch?"

THE YELLOW JACKET

An old farmer who was making a visit to the outhouse, happened to have the misfortune to receive a yellowjacket sting on the head of his private parts. It swelled up to twice the normal size. He didn't notice, but his wife took quite a liking to his new appendage. One morning the following week he happened to wake up just in time to see her getting ready to drop another yellow jacket on his equipment.

THE MINISTERIAL ASSOCIATION

A small town only had four churches, so it wasn't long after a ministerial association was formed until they really had little to talk about and were seriously considering disbanding. As a last desperate measure, one of the pastors suggested making the meetings more interesting. When asked what he had in mind, he suggested that at the following meeting, each of them would confess their one secret sin. As the next meeting unfolded, they took turns telling their darkest secrets. The Baptist minister confessed to sending the wife and kids off to visit the in-laws, at which time he drove to another town where nobody knew him, and bought beer and whiskey. The Methodist minister admitted to using the same visit the in-law ploy, only he went to strange towns and rented pornographic movies. The catholic priest admitted to vacation trips to Nevada to take advantage of the legal prostitution. Then all eyes were on the Presbyterian member, he suddenly announced that he just couldn't confess his secret sin. This brought so much anger from the remaining members that he relented. He stated, "my secret sin is gossip, and I can't wait to get out of here."

THE FOUR MOST DREADED WORDS

"Is it in yet?"

MARRIAGE

Marriage is like taking a bath, it's not so hot once you get used to it.

WRITE THREE LETTERS

A young man had just been selected as the city manager in a small rural town. As he entered his new office, his predecessor was just finishing cleaning his belongings out of the desk. They shook hands and as the old manager was going out the door, he told the new guy that he had left three numbered letters in the top left drawer. He explained that the first time he was in serious trouble with the city council, he should open the first letter. The next time he found himself in hot water, he should open the second letter. He said to hang on to the third letter until he was sure he was losing his job.

About half way through his third year in the job, the councilors were getting down on him, and he needed a way out. He remembered the letters, and went into his office and opened the first letter. It said simply, "Blame the previous administration." He tried the ploy and it worked. Everything went well for another year, at which time he once again found himself in hot water. He opened the second letter which only contained one word, "Reorganize" Reorganizing his operation worked like a charm, and all went well until after elections had changed the local City council, he found himself in ever deepening hot water. Finally, on his lunch break one day, he couldn't avoid it any longer and opened the third letter. It contained a one-word sentence, "Write three letters".

 HERMAPHRODITE

A hermaphrodite is a bi-sexual built for two.

NEW GUY IN TOWN

It was the early sixties, in a small town out in the wheat lands of North Central Oregon. It was one of those small towns that always keeps an unchanging population. Every time that some young lady had a baby, some guy left town. A quiet young man moved into town to accept a job at the local bank. On his first Sunday in town, he decided to attend church in hopes of making friends. The minister watched closely as the collection plated was passed, and noticed that the newcomer put $20 in the plate. At the start of the service, he asked the young man to stand up and introduce himself, and said as a reward for his freewill gift, he would be allowed to pick the first three hymns. He looked around and hesitated for a few seconds before announcing, "I'll take him, him, and him."

A RIDDLE

What goes "Clippity clop, Clippity Clop, Clippity Clop", then "Bang, Bang, Bang, Clippity Clop, Clippity Clop, Clippity Clop.""

Answer: An Amish drive by shooting.

WASTE NOT, WANT NOT

The reason that they stopped sacrificing virgins.

SUMMER AT UNCLE JACK'S

A young lad had just returned home from summer vacation at his slightly eccentric uncles' house that was located next to a lake. When asked about the summer's activities, he told his mom that the hardest part of the summer was in the evenings when his uncle would row him out the middle of the lake, and make him swim back to shore. His mom commented, "That must have been very hard for someone your age." To which the kid replied, "The hard part was getting out of the sack."

BAD SHROOMS

A man was taking a leisurely stroll through a local cemetery, when he noticed a man who seemed deep in thought as he knelt by one of the graves. He left a bouquet of flowers, then proceeded to another gravesite and repeated the same sequence. He couldn't help himself not to ask the man about who were the two deceased people that he seemed so attached to. The man explained that the first one was his second wife. When asked how she had passed away, he answered, "She died from eating poisonous mushrooms." When asked about the other gravesite, he said that she also died from eating poisonous mushrooms. When asked how many times the man had been married, he answered that he had been married 3 times. When asked if wife number 3 was still alive, he said that she had been the first one to expire, and she was buried a little further up the pathway. When asked if she had also eaten mushrooms, he answered that she had died of massive head trauma and then added, "She wouldn't eat the damned mushrooms."

I'LL TAKE THE SOUP

One afternoon at the nursing home, one of the elderly ladies started pulling her dress up over her head and shouting, "Super pussy", Two elderly gentlemen were watching the proceedings, and one asked the other, "What did she say? His friend said, "She said "Super pussy." After a few seconds the first man responded, "I'll take the soup."

WINDY DAY

A middle-aged woman was walking down a city street one afternoon, when a sudden gust of wind blew her skirt up over her head. She used both hands to keep her hat from blowing away. A man also walking along the sidewalk asked why she hung on to the hat instead of pulling her dress down. She replied, it's a new hat and what you were looking at is 56 years old.

A WISER OWL

Two owls were flying over the city on a blustery day, looking for shelter from the weather. One pointed out a window sill that might be a good place to take shelter. The other owl stated, "I lit on that sill one day and have never been the same since." It turned out that that particular window was for a doctor's office. When the owl last visited the window sill, the doctor was fresh from internship and had no clientele built up. Using the owl for practice he removed the bird's tonsils and hemorrhoids. As the owl explained, "I haven't been able to hoot worth a shit, or shit worth a hoot since."

3 RETIRED TRUCKERS

There were three truckers who had known each other for many years, and upon retiring each bought their own truck and became owner operators. One day they all happened to stop at the same truck stop for lunch. After lunch they went out to the parking lot and walked up to their trucks. The first new owner operator, had been very careful with his money and now owned a nearly new Kenworth conventional with lots of chrome and twin exhaust stacks. Always a show off, when he got to his truck, he opened the driver's side door, and reached under the driver's seat and produced a bottle of fine champagne. Holding the bottle aloft, he smashed the bottle over the shiny chrome bumper of his truck, and proclaimed, "I hereby christen this truck George Washington in honor of the Father of our Country." No to be outdone, the second driver reached behind the driver's seat of his 6 year old Peterbilt, and drug out half a bottle of Jack Daniel's Tennessee whisky, and upon smashing the bottle over his painted bumper, exclaimed, "I hereby christen this truck, Abraham Lincoln in honor of the Great Emancipator." The third driver didn't want to be left out, so he reached under the drivers seat of his ancient Freightliner cabover, pulled out a warm beer, and chugged it in one swallow, pissed on the half bumper that still adorned the front of the truck, and announced, "I hereby name this truck Teddy Roosevelt, because it's a rough riding son-of-a-bitch."

UNIVERSAL TRUTH

A woman is as old as she looks, but a man isn't old until he stops looking.

EVEN CHANGE

A man is leaving a deposit to nature, in a booth in a men's room, when a voice from the next booth inquired if there was any paper in that booth, the man notices for the first time that there isn't any paper there either, so answers in the negative. A couple minutes later another question comes from the adjoining booth. "Can you give me 5 ones for a five?

WALT DISNEY'S WORST NIGHTMARE

Snow white in the toy box, sitting on Pinocchio's face, saying, "Lie you son of a bitch, lie."

ROUNDABOUT REVENGE

A teenager walks into a house of ill repute, one afternoon and inquired as to whether they might have a girl with VD. The madam was shocked and asked why he wanted VD. He answered that he wanted to give it to his sister, the madam aske why he hated his sister so much, and he replied that he got along great with her, she would give it to his dad. He didn't hate his father either, he just wanted him to give it to his mom. So, after being asked if that wasn't a roundabout way to get his own mother infected. He said, there's no problem with mom, but she will give it to the milkman, and that's the son of a bitch that backed over, my bike.

WON'T SEE FOR FOUR DAYS

A couple had been married for a lot of years, and every year the fights seemed to get closer together and more intense. One evening he announced that he was going out by himself for the evening. She said that he most certainly was not. As she stood in front door blocking his path, he told her that if she did not move, she wouldn't see him for five days. She did not move, and anyway she proved him wrong, because she could see out of her right eye in only 3 days.

 # TINY AND GREEN

Question: What's tiny and green and smells like miss piggy?
   Answer: Kermit's finger.

HEARD ON THE CB

A driver had just gone to his doctor for his yearly physical. After giving him a thorough exam, he told him that he needed to quit drinking, smoking, driving such long hours, and eat healthier. When asked if it would make him live longer, the doctor told him, no, but said it would seem longer

RETURN TO THE JUNGLE

Did you hear about the cannibal that passed his brother in the forest?

OLD-OLD JOKE

Two young kids were sitting on the curb playing in the gutter when two men came walking by. One turned to the other and asked, "You got two dollars?" his companion answered in the affirmative. The first guy says, "Lets go across the street to the cathouse and get some nooky?" One kid turns to the other and said, What's nooky? As neither had a clue, they decided to wait for the two men to emerge and see how they looked. In a little while the two emerged all smiles and looked pretty happy. One kid turns to the other and asks, "you got any money, I've got a quarter." The other kid said that he had the same, they decided to cross the street and see what it was all about. The entered into a dimly lit room and immediately was confronted by an unhappy woman wearing a robe. She asked them what they wanted, they told her that they were after some nooky. She asked about money and they both handed her the quarters. She placed the money in the pocket of her robe, opened the robe, grabbed the first kid and rubbed his nose in her crotch, then grabbed the second kid and gave the him kid the same treatment. The kids wasted no time running back across the street. "Wow," said one of the boys, "I am so glad." When asked why that had made him glad, he said, "I just glad I didn't have two dollars".

CAMP CAMEL

A man had been out in the Arabian desert for a few months, so one day went up to the boss and asked what they did for sex out there. Without saying a word, the boss pointed at a camel in a small pen. The man allowed that although he had been out there quite a while, he hadn't been there that long. Two weeks later, went to the boss and told of his desire to use the camel. The boss took him over to the pen, and showed him the halter that was hanging there. The boss looked on in surprise as the guy tied the camel to the fence and had his way with it. When he returned to the boss, and noticing the stunned look on his face, asked, "Isn't that what the other guys do?" The boss told him that everybody else rode the camel over the next big dune to town.

CONVICT BROTHER

A man received a letter from his older brother, who had spent the last 20 years in prison. He was being released in a few days and asked if the man could come and pick him up at the prison. He found a place for his brother to live within walking distance of his home, and made reservations for them both on the train. On his way to the prison, he became concerned that his brother had not had any contact with women for twenty years. His concern was that he may have to restrain him if he created a scene when encountering a female. Everything went fine at first, but soon two young women came strolling past. His brother paid them no attention, then an attractive woman walked by and smiled at them. He asked his brother if he noticed the pretty lady, and he seemed unconcerned. He asked the brother if he thought her to be attractive. The brother allowed he guessed that she was OK, then blurted out, "But did you notice the ass on that conductor?"

THE BRIDGE BUILDER

A man is strolling through a city park one afternoon, he happened to notice a man sitting on a bench, and thought that he was the most dejected human being he had ever seen. Thinking that he might be able to cheer the man up, he walked over and said, "You got troubles, buddy?" The man nodded, and when asked if he wanted to talk about it, he pointed down the street to a bridge. "See that bridge?" He asked. When the second man nodded in agreement. He stated, "I designed that bridge and supervised the construction of it, but do they call me Jack the bridge builder?" "Hell, no!", "See that building 2 blocks down the street?" "I designed that, supervised the construction, but do they call me Jack the skyscraper builder?" "Hell no, but just suck one cock."

STRANGE PEPPER

Two elderly ladies were having tea one afternoon, when during a lull in the conversation, one turned to her friend and admitted that lately every time she sneezed, she had an orgasm. "My dear, what are you taking for it? She was asked. "Pepper, she replied."

TRUCK STOP GRAFFITI

Most of these are at least thirty years old, but probably have not improved with age.

Seen above a urinal, "Don't look up here, the joke is in your hand."

Also, above a urinal, "As I stand here trying to piss, I think of the girl who gave me this, if she's around when I get well, I'll catch it again sure as hell."

Nixon saw Deep Throat four times before he got it down Pat". (most folks are too young to make that one work.")

"My mother made me a homosexual"

Under that was written, "If I buy the yarn, will she make me one too?"

Bathroom stalls also got their fair share.

"Here I sit upon the pooper, giving birth to another state trooper".

"Here I sit with a broken heart, took two pills, now my truck won't start."

"Here I sit broken hearted, came to shit and only farted."

 ## QUESTION

Do you know the difference between a hard sleeper and a light sleeper?

A light sleeper sleeps with a light on.

FOOTBALL QUESTION

A young lady once asked her boyfriend if a lot of football players were gay. When he asked her why she wondered about that? She pointed at the TV and stated, "on that last play, they called one guy a tight end, and that other one, a wide receiver."

SCARING THE KIDS

A man came home from work early one afternoon, and ran upstairs to the bedroom. He opened the door and there on the bed was his wife, stark naked, and obviously in a state of distress. "What's going on in here?" he demanded, his wife said she was possibly having a heart attack. He bolted back down the stairs to call an ambulance. As he reached the living room, his son told him that there was a naked man in the closet. He yanked open the closet door, and there was his best buddy, trying to cover himself with a towel. "Dammit, Freddy", he shouted, "my wife's upstairs having a heart attack and you're down here scaring my kids".

CAT, NOT CALF

A farmer called the veterinarian and told him that he had a cat that seemed to be constipated. The vet. Told him that there would be a prescription waiting for him at the front desk. He read the instructions, which stated to give the cat one teaspoon of the medicine before going to bed that evening. The following morning the vet called and asked how the patient was doing. The farmer said that he couldn't believe how hard it was to get the medicine down the cat. "Cat?', I thought you said calf." Then enquired about the cat. "Well", said the farmer about an hour ago I saw the cat with five other cats out in the back pasture, they had three cats digging holes and two more covering."

WHERE ARE YOUR BALLS?

This one I heard while watching Redd Foxx on TV, during the Nixon years.

The President was honoring two Vietnam war heroes, and asked the first one what the country could do to repay his service. He answered that he would like to have 40 acres and a tractor. The President said that that would indeed happen. He asked the same question to the second vet., who said all he wanted was $2 for every inch between the head of his privates and his balls. The President was stunned by the request, but instructed the Surgeon General to measure the man on the spot. The Attorney General began to measure. After counting to six, he exclaimed, "Where are your balls?" To which the soldier replied, "South Vietnam."

GOOD NIGHT MOTHER OF FOUR

A man used to spend nearly every evening out drinking with his buddies. One evening as he was leaving for the bar, he turned to his wife, and said, "Goodnight mother of four." To which she replied, "Goodnight father of two." He never went out by himself again.

FALLING IRON WORKER

A team of ironworkers were working building a structure attached to the top of one of the tallest skyscrapers on earth. One of the men went up to the foreman, and explained that he had get rid of the morning's coffee. The foreman told him that it would take too long and they needed him, and wouldn't disrupt their schedule for something relatively minor like that. The worker said that he had waited until the last minute, and therefore wouldn't be able to hold it much longer. The foreman told him of an old trick that could be used in a situation like that. He explained that with the elevation of the building and the ambient temperature, which was above 90 degrees, the urine would evaporate before it hit the street below. He picked up a heavy plank and laid it down with the end protruding three feet out over the edge of the building, he offered to stand on the other end to counterbalance the weight of the worker. Everything went well until the Foreman got a call on his cell phone, and forgot what he was doing at that moment, and turned around and walked off. The iron worker plunged to the street below, and a major investigation followed. When they interviewed witnesses in the offices below who had seen or heard anything, one man said that he thought it was sex related. When asked why he thought so, he said that as the man was falling, he heard him yell, "Where did you go you cocksucker?"

THE WAY IT USED TO BE

In the "good ol' days, many young men went out on Saturday night and sowed their wild oats, then went to church on Sunday and prayed for crop failure.

LADY COVINGTON

A man was flying to England. He had totally burned out his short-term memory as a young man after taking LSD, so had resorted to keeping a large notebook in which he detailed everything he did. The man in the seat beside him decided to engage in some small talk to alleviate the boredom. He asked whether the man had been to England before. He opened his notebook, and looked up travel. "Yes", he responded, "I have been there before". The man asked next if he had met a woman named Lady Covington. After searching his book for acquaintances, he replied that he had indeed been introduced to her. The man asked next if by any chance had he had an affair with her. This prompted him to research the affair section of the book. After closing the book, he replied that yes indeed, he had had an affair with her. His seatmate then stated, "I am Lord Covington and I don't like that one bit." He went back to the book under opinions, and then stated, "Neither did I."

OPINION

If you think that sex is a pain in the ass, you might be doing it wrong.

POLAR BEAR

One day during lunch hour, one of the guys turned the man next to him and asked, "what do polar bears do?" the man replied, "as far as I know, all they do is sit out on the ice and eat seals and raw fish." The first man allowed as he was going to hate that. When asked what he was talking about, he replied that one of his friends had passed away, and he had been asked to be a polar bear.

THE NEW ALASKAN

This goes back to the very early '60's when Alaska and Hawaii achieved statehood.

A Texas oilman was extremely unhappy about Alaska now being the largest state, He stewed over it for a considerable time before finally deciding to move to Alaska. He flew into Anchorage and took a taxi to the nearest bar. Once in the bar he explained his goal to the bartender, and asked if there was any official method of becoming a real Alaskan. The bartender decided to mess with him a little bit, so told him that he only had to do three things, to be approved for residency. When asked what those things were, he was informed that he would have to drink a fifth of whiskey all in one drink, make love to a beautiful Eskimo maiden, and shoot a Polar Bear through the heart. He wasted no time in buying the whisky, and somehow getting it all down in one drink. After a few minutes, he launched himself toward the front door. It took him three tries to get out the door, and he staggered up the street. The bartender was pretty sure that he wouldn't be seeing him again. To his amazement, a few hours later the Texan returned. He looked like he had been mauled by a pack of rabid wolves, he had very few square inches of skin that weren't bleeding. He looked at the bartender and asked, "Alright, where's that Eskimo I gotta shoot?

THE PRESIDENT PLAYS GOLF

Former President Nixon was playing a round of golf with former basketball great, Wilt Chamberlin. After the game was concluded, they went to the locker room, showered and were getting dressed when the President said, "Excuse me Wilt, but I can't help noticing that you are quite well endowed, is there anything that you do to enhance that growth?" Wilt admitted that every night before getting into bed, he rapped it on the head of the bed a few times before climbing in. When the Pres got to bed that night it was quite late, and just before he got into bed, he had to stand really close, but managed to rap the bedpost two or three times. Pat suddenly sat up in bed and asked, "Wilt, is that you?"

MORE TRUCK STOP GRAFFITI

"Nixon saw Deep Throat four times before he got it down Pat.

CHANGE IN FASHION

A guy had just finished a round of golf with and old golfing buddy and as they were changing back into street clothes, he couldn't help but notice that his friend was trying to put on a lady's girdle. Being quite curious, he couldn't help asking how long he had been wearing the girdle. His friend replied that it was ever since his wife had found it under the front seat of his car.

AGE & TREACHERY OVERCOMES YOUTH & SKILL

A new young rooster had just been introduced to the barnyard. The old "past his prime" rooster went up to introduce himself. He suggested that they could split the hens 50 – 50, to which the young rooster told him to get lost because the hens were all his. The old guy suggested that he could at least keep five for himself. Once more he was told that they all belonged to the new rooster. As one last try, he asked for just one for himself and received the same answer. As a last resort, he proposed a footrace around the barn, but stipulated that he would need a sizable head start due to his advanced age, to which the young rooster laughingly agreed. The old rooster limped about 50 feet, then started hopping around the barn. The young rooster gave him a little more time and then started leisurely running to catch up. As they rounded the back side of the barn, the young rooster was within just a few feet of overtaking the hopping, wheezing older bird. Just then a shotgun barrel came around the corner of the barn and killed the young bird instantly. The farmer then exclaimed, "Dammit, that's the third gay rooster I've bought this Summer".

FAVORITE THING

A Chinese man visited America, and upon returning home was asked what he liked best during his visit. He replied that he enjoyed watching a game called "Aw shit.' People would sit around tables, with cards and beans in front of them. Numbers were called and then someone yelled "Bingo" and everybody else said, "Aw Shit."

THE VERY FIRST

Two elderly ladies were best friends and spent many afternoons rocking in their rockers and reminiscing about times past and stories about relatives both past and present. At times they would enhance stories in a game of one-upmanship. One day when discussing older generations, one related a tale about her uncle who was one of the first electricians in the State of Oklahoma. He had won a government contract to electrify a modern restroom on an Indian reservation. Her friend was not terribly impressed by the story and asked what kind of impression that was supposed to make on history. Her friend replied, don't you understand? "My uncle was the first man in America to wire a head for a reservation."

SUREFIRE COUGH REMEDY

This is from the early '60's (in case you don't recognize the product.)
Ex-Lax and hot water, you don't dare cough.

A TIME TO RUN

A grizzled old sailor wandered into a sporting house in the Far East. As he entered, he was escorted to a room by a young woman who took off her robe and turned to the old guy, and said, "I give you something you never had before, G.I." The old "salt" then ran out of the room screaming, "Leprosy, Leprosy!!!

BEAR POOP

A young man was hitch-hiking through the mountains of Montana one summer. As he walked along the street in a small rural town surrounded by mountains, he noticed that a lot of the people he met on the street had little silver bells attached to their clothing. Finally, he noticed an older gentleman wearing a uniform that he took to be a forest ranger. As they met, he excused himself and asked if the ranger could explain the mystery to him. With a chuckle, the older gentleman explained. "A lot of these tourists have talked to "wildlife experts", who think that bears won't attack if they are not surprised". If you look closely, they will have a bulge in their jacket that contains pepper spray, or carry it on their belts. The pepper spray is supposed to ward off the bear in case it doesn't hear the bells and attacks anyway. He asked what was the best way to stay away from bears, as he wanted to hike in the mountains and stay as safe as possible. The old gentleman told him to be aware of his surroundings, and if he saw bear poop to be especially careful, and he said to make sure what kind of bear the poop belonged to. When asked how to tell the difference, he was told that if the poop was about a handful, and had berries in it, it was black bear poop and unless it was a female with young cubs, was not normally dangerous. If, on the other hand, the pile of poop was much larger and smelled of pepper, and contained small silver bells, if was a grizzly, and to get the Hell out of there.

BAD NEWS BADLY DONE

A logger named Wilson was killed on the job one day and the newest member of the crew was appointed to inform the new widow about the accident. He drove to the address and walked up and knocked on the door. The door opened and he said, "Are you the widow Wilson?" When she answered in the negative, he replied, "You wanna bet?"

WRONG ORDER

A traveling survey crew were working in the wilds of Canada when they encountered a small river which they hadn't anticipated, on their next trip to town, they sent a telegram to headquarters, requesting two punts and a canoe. They received an answering telegram which read, the girls arrive next Tuesday, what the hell is a panoe?

PURPLE JOKES

Q: What was purple, and conquered the World"
  A: Alexander the grape.
  Q: What's purple and stamps out forest fires?
  A: Smokey the grape.
  Q: What did the grape say when the elephant stepped on Him?
  A: Nothing, he just let out a little wine.

# LITTLE JOHNNY JOKES

These were really popular during the early to mid-sixties.

The teacher avoided calling on little Johnny because he always said something vulgar every time, he opened his mouth. One morning she asked if anyone in the class could use the word "beautiful" in a sentence. To her chagrin, the only hand in the air was attached to Johnny. After hoping for another volunteer, she reluctantly called on him. Johnny stood up and said, "This morning at breakfast, my sister said she was pregnant, and my dad said, "beautiful, f**kin' beautiful."

The teacher decided to spice up the morning in the classroom with a class participation exercise. She announced that at the start of every morning, she would ask a question, and if anyone could come up with the correct answer, they could have the rest of the day off, as well as the following day. The first day, she asked how many gallons of water in the ocean, Followed the following day with, how high is the sky? By Friday morning, Johnny was ready for her. He had taken two golf balls and painted them brown. Just as the teacher cleared her throat to ask the question of the day, he rolled the balls down the aisle directly toward her. She paused and then asked, "OK, who's the comedian with the brown balls?" The question was fielded by Jonny, who proclaimed, "Bill Cosby, see ya Friday" and walked out.

One morning the teacher asked if anyone could express optimism in a single sentence. The first one to raise her hand, was called to the front of the room to tell the whole class. She stated, "My name is

Sadie, and I want to grow up to be a lady, and have a baby, if I can, and I think I can." Once more, the only other volunteer was Johnny, with apprehension, she called on him, and he addressed the class, "My name is Johnny, and I want to grow up to be a man, and help little Sadie with her plan, if I can, and I think I can".

One morning, she asked if anyone could come up with a sentence the described action. And once more the only hand raised was Johnny. Reluctantly she asked him to come to the front of the room and recite his sentence. He started with, "One day I saw a cockroach run up the wall." The teacher commented, "Johnny, try that one more time but this time leave the "cock" out." "OK" said Johnny, "A cockroach ran up the wall, with his cock out."

21 DAY CAMEL

A famous explorer once discovered some very important relics out in the wilds of the Arabian desert. Upon returning to civilization, he found that the only possible way to transport the treasure back to town was by camel. Upon enquiring on renting camels, he discovered that none of the camel owners were willing to rent their camels to him due to the fact that the treasure site was as at least a 20-day round trip, and camels could only go 19 days without water. One afternoon as he sat on a bench under a palm tree trying to come up with a way to transport the relics, he was approached by an old man who told him that there was a way that the camels could be made able to extend the trip to at least 21 days. When asked what the plan would entail, the old man told him to rent the camels, and then hold them for 19 days without water, and then lead them one at a time to the water. The only equipment needed would be a pair of bricks. When asked to explain the plan, the old man told him to take the thirsty camel to the water, and let the animal drink. The camel would drink until it had reached its limit, and then would raise its head, then lower its head one last time and sniff the water. Standing behind the camel, he would slam the two bricks together on the animal's nuts, and the camel would inhale two more days of water.

 SIGN LANGUAGE

One afternoon in a small tavern in an equally small community, the bartender, who was newly hired, watched an elderly gentleman walk through the front door and approach the bar. The bartender inquired what the old gentleman wanted to drink, then realized that his customer was unable to speak. The old guy had played this charade many times, and held out his right hand like making the "OK" sign, and then pointed his left index finger toward the center of the index finger and thumb of the other hand. Just as he was inches away, just before reaching the target, he bent the approaching finger as though he had missed the target. A customer seated a short way down the bar noticed the perplexed look on the face of the bartender, and exclaimed, "He comes in here all the time, and he drinks Old Grandad."

THE GOLDEN COMMODE

A man comes downstairs one morning and notices that his roommate looks like he has one of the World's worst hangovers. He had noticed that he had come in pretty late the evening before and asked for details of his excursion. The roommate told him that there was a new nightclub in town that was one of the swankiest places he had ever been in his whole life. He said that the parking lot was at least two acres in size, that the bar was 100 feet long, and there were bartenders every 10 feet. He then related that they had a full orchestra for live entertainment. He stated that the best part of the elegance was the golden commode in the men's room. The roommate asked the name of the place, and then waited for his buddy to leave for work. After finding the phone number for the new establishment, he called to see if indeed the new place did indeed have everything he had been told about. The bartender confirmed all the details until it came to the golden commode. At that point he said, "Just a minute" and then with his hand only partly over the receiver, hollered, "Hey Eddie, I think I have a line on the guy that shit in your tuba."

WHAT?

A young couple had been married for three years and had already wound up with three little ones. Deciding to take some preventative measure to stop the process, they went to see their family doctor. He gave both a thorough exam., he fitted the wife with a hearing aid. It seemed that every night before retiring for the night, he would ask if she wanted to go to sleep or what. She would reply, "What?"

CHARM SCHOOL

A young woman was being bored by a neighbor, who regaled her to no end about how wonderful her new kitchen, new carpet, new car, and other inane details, to which she replied "How nice, "after each item was recited. After a short pause, the neighbor asked what was new in her life. She responded that her husband had recently sent her to charm school. The neighbor thought that to be rather strange, but merely asked what she had learned. She replied that the main difference was that when she was being bored by inane conversation, she responded by saying, "How nice." Instead of "Bullshit".

 DEFINITION

The new definition of "Total rejection", is when you're playing with yourself and your hand falls asleep.

THE CARNIVAL

A young lady was on a blind date when the travelling carnival came to town. Her date asked her what she liked, she answered that she wanted to be weighed. Dutifully he escorted her to the man who guessed weight, who guessed her at 123 lbs. A little later he again asked what she would like to do, and again she asked to be weighed. Ignoring the looks from the weight guesser, he once more pronounced her at 123 pounds. Her date thought that there must be something terribly wrong with her, and not long later took her back home. As she entered her home, her mother asked how her date had gone, to which she replied, "It was wousy".

BAD NEWS

A young man came down with a rare form of venereal disease. He went to four doctors, all of whom declared that they had never seen anything like it, and that amputation would be the only treatment that would solve the issue. Finally, in desperation he contacted an oriental doctor, hoping against hope, that he might be acquainted with the malady. After a brief examination, the doctor said that he hadn't seen that condition for many years. He asked if the young man had been to American doctors, and after confirmation, asked if they had told him that amputation was the only answer. He replied that they all had indeed said that very thing. The doctor chuckled and replied, "Those American doctors, all they think of is money, you wait two more weeks, and it will fall off by itself."

THE FOXHOLE

During a lull in the action, two soldiers were dispatched with shovels to bury a mule that had died two days before. As they are digging, they get into a disagreement about exactly what was the name of the animal they were burying. One said it was a mule, while the other maintained that it was an ass. They bet $2 on the outcome and agreed that the first person they saw would decide which was in the right. A short time later a chaplain drove up in a jeep, and when queried about the true name of the beast, declared that according to scripture it was an ass. A while later a jeep approached and stopped and the driver asked if they were digging a foxhole. The loser of the bet stated, "Not according to scripture."

THE NEW BULL

Two range bulls were lying in the shade of a nearby tree. They would be herded out the Summer range soon. A while later they noticed a cattle truck coming up the lane to the barn. As they watched a new bull was unloaded. To their alarm, the bull was a huge Brahma, and appeared to have a bad temper. As soon as he was unloaded, he started bellowing and pawing dirt into the air. One of the older bulls jumped to his feet, started doing some bellowing and dirt slinging of his own. The other bull asked him if he was trying to get them both killed. His companion told him that he wanted to make sure the new bull knew that he was a bull.

PEARL

(I love this joke, but if it's too politically incorrect we can leave it out.)

Did you ever hear about the young man who was half black, and half Japanese? Every December 7th he attacked Pearl Bailey.

YOU MIGHT HAVE A SKI LOOSE

A young couple timed their wedding to allow them to go on a skiing honeymoon. On the first morning, they overslept, and were certain that everyone else in the hotel were aware that they were newlyweds, and would tease them unmercifully about being up so late in the morning. The groom came up with a way to make it looked like they had gotten up ahead of all the other skiers, and were the first to head out to the slopes. The tossed all their gear out of the hotel window, and followed by jumping out themselves, wearing all their ski gear. They rolled in the snow, and then surprised everyone in the lodge by making a grand entrance into the lobby. When asked how they were enjoying the honeymoon, the groom exclaimed, "Anybody that doesn't like to screw, has a ski loose."

HONEYMOONERS

A newly married young couple had rented a room from a farmer, who had converted the loft in his barn into a nice cozy bedroom. After two days of not seeing the couple, even at mealtime, the farmer decided that he should check on them. Standing under the window to the bedroom, he tossed a couple small stones at said window. The bridegroom poked his head out the window, and when asked if they planned to come down for dinner, he stated that they were living on the fruits of love, the farmer replied that he wished they wouldn't throw the peelings out the window, as they were killing his chickens.

WHAT'S WITH THE BOWLING BALL?

A deeply religious, and naïve young couple had just gotten married. Just before leaving for their honeymoon, the father of the groom took his son aside, and knowing the depth of his son's innocence, gave him some quick advice. He told the young man that when they went to bed to put the hardest thing he had into where she went potty. The following morning as the couple were lying in bed, she told him that she still didn't understand why he put the bowling ball in the toilet.

Printed in the United States
By Bookmasters